THE ULTIMATE **SPY** CLUB

T5-CCV-764

PROTECTING YOUR ROOM, YOUR STUFF & YOUR SECRETS

by **Suzanne Francis**

with **Tony and Jonna Mendez**
Consultants

Scholastic Inc.

New York • Toronto • London • Auckland • Sydney
Mexico City • New Delhi • Hong Kong • Buenos Aires

ISBN 0-439-89770-X
Copyright © 2006 by Scholastic Inc.

Designer: Aruna Goldstein
Illustrations: James W. Elston
Comic Strip Illustrations: Yancey Labat

Photos: Page 9: Bettman/Corbis. Page 10: popperfoto.com.
Page 11: Library of Congress. Page 13: From the Public Domain.
Page 14: popperfoto.com. Page 23: AFP/Getty Images.
Page 28: Markowitz Jeffrey/Corbis Sygma.

For information regarding permission, write to Scholastic Inc., Attention:
Permissions Department, 557 Broadway, New York, NY 10012.
SCHOLASTIC, THE ULTIMATE SPY CLUB, and associated logos are
trademarks and/or registered trademarks of Scholastic Inc.

12 11 10 9 8 7 6 5 4 3 2

6 7 8 9 10 11/0

Printed in the U.S.A.

First printing, October 2006

Table of Contents

Welcome, Trainee

Tired of your little sib messing around with your stuff? Trying to figure out who keeps busting into your backpack? Sounds like you need to polish up your spy skills and tighten up security!

Just about everything a spy does is secret, so incorporating top-notch security measures into your everyday life is crucial. A sloppy spy runs the risk of having his or her secrets leaked out, intercepted, or discovered by the enemy.

Just like a spy, you need to know how to keep your space, your gear, and your secrets safe whether you're at home, in school, or on the go. Well, fear not—you're about to learn all kinds of cool spy tips and tricks to do just that. With your new **Ultimate Spy Club** handbook and the spy gadgets in your kit, you'll learn about...

Alarms

Alarms can protect a spy's top-secret things when they're not around. Spies should always be able to set up an alarm—no matter where they are or what materials they have on hand. You'll learn how to make your own alarms and put them to use so you'll always be secure.

Traps

Traps are a great way to catch a snoop. Some traps are silent and sneaky, so the snoop never even realizes they've been caught. Being a spy is all about information, and you'll get the 411 on how to set all kinds of traps—even a trap that uses nothing more than one tiny hair!

Secret Hiding Places

What's a surefire way to keep your toys, your notes, and your spy gear safe from snooping peeps? Great hiding spots! By hiding your stuff, you keep it safe and sound because snoops don't even know it's there. You'll get ideas for lots of clever places to hide things so you can keep your enemies as clueless as possible.

And more!

Be sure to visit the
Ultimate Spy Club online at:
www.scholastic.com/ultimatespy

This month's secret password is:
safeandsound

5

What's in Your *Spy Kit*?

Your spy kit includes three Ultimate Spy Club gadgets:

Motion Detector and Decoy Covers

Using a special light sensor, this motion detector will let you know if someone is entering a space that you want to keep protected. Your alarm comes with two decoy covers so you can fool counterspies and nosy snoops. They'll never suspect it!

Binder Lock with Card Keys

Attach your binder lock to any binder or notebook to keep it secure. The only way to open this lock is with your card keys, so don't lose 'em! With your private journal or mission log locked up tight, the snoops don't stand a chance.

Invisible Ink Pens

No one will be able to see the messages you write with these pens, because the ink is invisible! Write with the blue end, then use the pen's special gray tip to reveal the secret message.

MISSION #1:
PROTECTING YOUR HQ

Just like every kid needs a room, every spy needs a headquarters (HQ) or **base of operations**—somewhere to talk to friends, do work, and keep your stuff. Basically, headquarters is like home—that's why it's sometimes called "home base." Even if a spy is on a mission away from home, he or she will find a temporary HQ called a **safe site** or **safe house**. Any way you cut it, a spy always needs a place to call home—er, headquarters!

Your HQ can be anywhere: your room, a clubhouse, a treehouse, or even a closet. But whatever location you choose for your HQ, you need to protect it. The last thing a spy wants is someone poking around or peeking into **classified** files, notebooks, or anything else top secret!

Real spies use all sorts of spy **tradecraft** like alarms and traps to guard their HQ and keep it a secret. How do they do it? Read on!

How Alarming!

BEEP! BEEP! BEEP!

SPY LOG

JUICE BOX

Alarms are a great way to keep your room safe from intruders. They let you know if anyone tries to sneak in whether you're there or not. Picture this: Your nosy sib is trying to get into your room to see your top-secret project. She opens the door ever so carefully and tiptoes inside. Then... BEEP! BEEP! BEEP! That juice box sitting on your desk is really an alarm, and it's caught her in the act!

Beep! Beep! Beep! You're Busted!

The motion detector from your spy kit is a great way to secure your space. Set up your motion detector *inside* your room so that anyone entering your room will set it off. Your motion detector works by detecting shadows, so it works best in a well-lit room. Anyone who casts a shadow on it will set off the alarm. Look around. Where would someone enter your room? Is there a certain area you need to keep safe?

And don't forget your decoys! Place the juice box or camera cover onto your motion detector. Nobody will suspect that those ordinary items are going to get them caught!

James Bond had his spy car, the Aston Martin DB-5. Maxwell Smart in *Get Smart* had his infamous shoe phone. These fictional secret agents used gizmos that *looked* like ordinary things but actually had multiple secret spy uses.

Your Eyes and Ears

What if you're inside your room working on a top-secret project? How can you make sure no one busts in and sees what you're working on? Try setting up your alarm outside your room to warn you if that snooping sib approaches. It's like having eyes outside the door! Make sure you put the alarm far enough from the entrance that you'll have time to hide your secrets if someone's coming! Stash them away and act natural. The snoop will never know what he missed.

SPY TIP:

What if you don't have access to your motion detector? Or what if there's more than one space to protect? No problem!

➥ Use a strong piece of thread to tie a bunch of empty cans or some bells together. String the cans or bells across the doorway or simply hang them inside your closed door. If someone tries to open the door— CLANG!

➥ Turn a sheet of bubble wrap into an instant alarm. Place the bubble wrap under a doormat or rug in front of your HQ. The cat will be too light to set it off, but an intruder will set off a loud popping noise, announcing his unwanted arrival.

KEEP OUT!

Super Spy Traps

Don't want to set up a loud alarm to snag an intruder? Maybe you're looking for something a bit more secretive. Try setting one of these five traps. You'll catch the trespasser and keep him in the dark.

Door Trap

Try setting a trap using your invisible ink pens. Secure a piece of paper under the door and use your invisible ink pen to mark where the edge of the door is.

When you return, take the reveal side of the pen and run it along the paper near the door. Do the mark and the door still line up? If not, you can be sure you had a visitor.

Hair Trap

Take a piece of hair or thread (three inches long) and wet it with water or some good old-fashioned spit. Close your bedroom door and stick the hair between the door and the doorjamb about one foot above the ground (that's low enough that no one will notice). If the hair is on the floor when you return, there's only one thing you can say: "Somebody's been hair!"

Pop Culture

In the movie *Dr. No*, James Bond, also known as agent 007, traps a door in his hotel room using a single hair from his head.

REAL SPY GADGETS

This is a letter found in George Washington's papers. It has a fake letter written in regular ink with a secret invisible-ink letter written upside down and backwards between the lines.

Real spies use invisible ink to write secret messages, and invisible detection powder called *spy dust* to catch snoops and counterspies. When the powder is dusted onto doorknobs and documents, it's invisible. But when someone touches it, the powder can be seen under ultraviolet light.

Powder Trap

Sprinkle a tiny trail of chalk dust or baby powder on the floor just inside your door. If anyone comes in, they'll leave footprints, smudges, and drag lines wherever they go. If the intruder decides to remove the evidence by dusting the surface completely, that will be your biggest clue of all. Dusted and busted!

Placement Trap

Arrange things in your room so you know exactly where they are—*and* if they've been moved. Align the edges of papers and books on your desk or use pencil tips to point at certain words. Write down all the clues you've left yourself. When you return, check out your setup. Have things been moved around?

Invisible Intelligence

Suspect someone's snooping around? Leave out an empty folder marked "top secret." Place a piece of paper under the bait and use your invisible ink pen to mark where the edges are. When you get back, use the reveal end of your pen to see if the folder was moved.

Alternate Spy HQ Ideas

If your bedroom just isn't private enough, no worries! Your HQ can be just about anywhere as long as it's safe and secure.

Use your imagination to think of places around your house that could make a good HQ. What about the basement? Or an empty closet? If you can't find a spot inside, take a peek outside. An old treehouse, toolshed, or garage might make a terrific spot for your headquarters. Here are some things to think about when searching for the perfect place to hang your badge.

A Little Privacy, Please!

You're going to be conducting secret business at your HQ, so you need to have privacy. You can't have people breezing in and out, or getting a view of top-secret plans. Think about ways to make your HQ more private. Try using rope, sheets, cardboard, newspapers, and masking tape to create "walls" around your space. If you're in a big space, think about sectioning off a small area to make it more manageable. Be sure to ask an adult first!

KEEP OUT!

KEEP OUT!

Keep Out!

Another way to ensure privacy is to control who comes in and out. You might not have a door with a lock, but that's okay—you can improvise! If the walls are cloth, the door may be a flap, like on a tent. If you are up in a treehouse, the door might be a board that closes off the top of the ladder. Outside, your HQ might be shielded from view by a row of plants. As long as you have some kind of "door," you're good to go!

REAL SPY GADGETS

CIA headquarters has tons of tip-top security. High fences, security guards, and alarms are just the beginning. The most secret stuff is kept in heavy metal safes with combination locks. All employees have special badges and all secret documents are carefully destroyed when they're no longer needed.

It's tough to copy these top security measures, but you can use some similar tactics. Set alarms in strategic places and make badges for you and your co-spies. Do what you can to keep your HQ safe!

THE KROGER SPY HOUSE

Peter and Helen Kroger, antiquarian booksellers in suburban London, England, were actually Morris and Lona Cohen— two American spies who were working for the Soviet Union. Their identity was really a **cover** to help them blend in and go about their spying without looking suspicious. They were part of a **spy network** called the Portland Spy Ring that helped pass information about the atomic bomb to the Soviet Union.

The Kroger headquarters was in a normal suburban house. When police searched the house, they found a trap door in the kitchen floor that led to a room where the Krogers stored all of their spy gear. The police found codebooks, microdots, ciphers, and quick-burning paper. They even found a radio transmitter hidden in a space heater!

Keeping Your HQ Secret

Since you'll be conducting secret activities at your headquarters, it's important to keep its location under wraps. You don't want anyone to notice you and your co-spies going to and from your HQ. That's why you need to develop a special **protocol** for getting there.

Crisscrossing Confusion

Instead of walking a direct path toward HQ, put a little zigzag into it. If your HQ is in the basement, map out a path that makes it look like you're going to the garage. Then at the last minute quickly duck down the stairs. If your HQ is in a treehouse, make it look like you're heading to the porch before you enter. Walk a crooked path, and you'll make your enemy spy's head spin!

Switch It Up

Are there different ways to get to your HQ? Try switching the route you take so people won't notice you're going to the same place over and over again.

Pop Culture

In the television show *Get Smart*, bumbling secret agent Maxwell Smart had amazing gadgets and a secret entrance to his spy headquarters. To get down to his hidden HQ, the secret agent went into a phone booth that was really an elevator!

Real spies sometimes use a *cover*, like a storefront, to disguise their offices. Can you think of ways to disguise your headquarters?

Off Your Tail

When you and your co-spies are heading to HQ, you should do an **SDR** or **Surveillance Detection Run**. That's what spies do to make sure they aren't being followed, or **tailed**. The challenge is not to look suspicious—otherwise the person following you will know they've been caught!

Make a habit of looking around all the time and taking note of who you see and what they're doing. Didn't your neighbor just mow his lawn yesterday? Could he be trying to look busy while spying on you?

Direction Protection

If you think there really is a spy on your tail, try switching directions a few times. Pretend you forgot something and turn back in the direction you came from— just act like you're lost and start walking the other way. If the suspect turns

around with you, you know he's a bit too interested in where you're going!

Storefront Snare

Another way to see if someone is following you is to walk up to a storefront with a large window. Casually act like you're looking at the display: "Huh. Those shoes are something else!" You're not really admiring the shoes (in fact, they're pretty ugly). You're checking out the reflection in the window to see if someone is behind you. You are one sly spy!

Security Breach

If a counterspy *does* manage to follow you to headquarters, should you give up and surrender? No way! Never! If someone discovers your secret HQ, the best thing to do is to send a **danger signal** to your co-spies. This means you'll need to set up some prearranged codes.

Secret Signals

Prearranged codes are like a secret language for you and your friends. Everyone in your network should know what each code means. Saying, "Pickles for lunch, please!" could mean, "There's a counterspy watching." You could be even sneakier and decide that using two *p*'s in a sentence is the signal. For example, "I could eat a pile of peanuts," and "I love pumpkin pie," would both mean, "There's a counterspy watching, so keep cool!"

Codes can be as simple as a single word, or not use words at all! You can hum a tune, come up with a snapping or knocking pattern, or use hand signals. Be sure to create codes for "Don't go back to HQ," "The coast is clear," "Danger," and "I'm calling a meeting," so every situation is covered. As long as everyone knows what the code means, you're set!

POP Culture

In the movie *Cats & Dogs*, the dogs are running surveillance on the cats. When one of the cats leaves the house, the dog radios to HQ and says, "The jelly is out of the doughnut." This prearranged code sweetly lets the other dogs know that the cat has left the premises.

MISSION #2:
PROTECTING YOUR STUFF

Need to keep your little sister or brother out of your stuff? Tired of your toys getting broken? You've got stuff in your house, at school, and in your backpack. How can you possibly protect it all? With a little spy know-how, keeping that stuff safe is a cinch!

Hide It

How do you conduct **counterintelligence** (protecting your gear from the enemy) when you're not home? Put your stuff right out of a snoop's sight by hiding it! Spies are always looking for terrific hiding places because they need lots of them.

Some of the best hiding places are right in front of your nose. Take a few minutes to look around. Everything you see is a potential hiding spot. What about that old lunch box in your closet? Can you stash a secret note behind the calendar on your wall? Get creative and see how many hiding places you can find.

Here are a few suggestions to get you started:

➡ A cigar box can be a great place for spy materials. Try covering the top of the box with the cover of an old book—that'll disguise it! With hiding spots, the less interesting, the better. That way you can be sure that nobody tries to "check out" your "book" when you're not looking.

➡ Use an old VCR, CD, or DVD case to hide your stuff. You can hide all kinds of documents and small toys inside, and then leave it on the shelf. No one will be suspicious.

➡ You can double security by using your binder lock on a special box or hollowed-out book. Attach the binder lock, then put it back onto the shelf with the unlocked side facing out.

Guard It

Your motion detector can help you keep your things safe too. Just set it up near your secret stash using one of your decoy disguises. When the sneaky snoop comes to grab your stuff, they'll get an earful!

School Security

You spend an awful lot of time at school, so you've got a lot of stuff there—in your desk, in your backpack, and more. How can you make sure it all stays safe? Try these tips and tricks, and you'll keep those curious classmates out.

Desk Trap

If you think someone's been messing with your desk, set a trap and find out for sure. Put two pieces of paper at the front of your desk. Hold the papers down and mark a stripe across both papers with your invisible ink pen. Remove your hands gently so you don't move the papers. Your trap is set. If a snoop comes a knockin', he'll have to move those papers—and that's what'll bust 'em. When you come back to your desk, don't move anything. Carefully hold the papers in place and use the reveal end of your pen to find the invisible ink. Does the line on both papers still line up? If not, someone's been in your desk!

Backpack Attack

You carry your backpack just about everywhere you go, and it usually contains more than a few important items. How can you keep track of it when you have to put it down? With the following tricks up your sleeve, the busybodies will have to busy themselves with someone else's biz!

⇨ Fasten a small bell to the inside of your backpack. When you take it to school, stuff a tissue into the bell to keep it from ringing. Once you put your backpack down, remove the tissue. Anybody touching your backpack will set off the bell. DING! DING!

⇨ Take a small piece of beeswax or scotch tape and place it over your zipped-up zipper. If that nosy classmate unzips your bag, the tape or wax will be broken—proof that she's not minding her own beeswax!

SPY TIP:

Keep your special stuff in a drawer? Try setting this trap using a little ol' toothpick. Wedge a wooden toothpick into the side of your drawer in the crack between the side of the desk or dresser and the drawer itself. After you've pushed it in as far as it will go, snap it in half. Your trap is set! If anyone opens the drawer, the small piece of toothpick will fall onto the floor. Nobody will notice but you!

REAL SPY GADGETS

When governments like the United States send secrets from one country to another, the documents are secured in heavy, bright-orange canvas bags called *diplomatic pouches*. These pouches are trapped with wax seals, special tape, and string. That way, the government will know if someone tried to open the pouch.

MISSION #3:
PROTECTING YOUR SECRETS

Spies constantly need to record **classified** information and relay it to the people who need to know. The trick is to keep it safe! Spies always need to be extra careful. They never know who's after the information they have or what could happen if it ends up in the wrong hands.

Here are a few handy ways to keep your information safe, write secret messages, pass them, and destroy the evidence!

Writing Secret Messages

You have an important secret note to write to your friend and you have to make sure that no one else sees it. How do you do it? Write the message with one of your invisible ink pens and make sure your friend has the other one. Have your friend read the message in a safe place, and mission accomplished!

SPY TIP:

Want to *really* throw off wandering eyes?

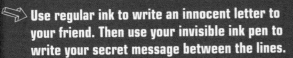 Use regular ink to write an innocent letter to your friend. Then use your invisible ink pen to write your secret message between the lines.

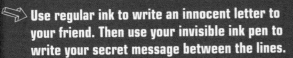 Or, make your message look like something that shouldn't be trashed—homework, notes, or phone numbers—so your secret invisible-ink note stays safe!

Hey!
Top-secret meeting at HQ
What's up? Nothing much going on
after school today.
Just wanted to say hi!

Invisible Espionage

Once you've got your hands on your enemy's plans, you'll need to keep their secrets safe as well. Say you overheard a group of enemy spies making a plan. What do you do?

Quickly pull out your invisible ink pen and jot down some notes on an innocent-looking piece of paper. If a **spotter** (an enemy spy who looks out for counterspies) wanders over, purposely reveal your social studies handout. He'll never know that his secret plan is carefully detailed on your homework sheet in invisible ink!

SPY HISTORY uNcovEREd

Josephine Baker was a famous American singer and dancer who became very popular in Paris in the 1920s. During World War II, she worked for the French Resistance, helping them fight against the Nazis. She would sneak important info out of France—often written on her sheet music in invisible ink! Since she was so famous, passport officials never thought to suspect her!

23

Passing Secret Messages

Now that your **classified** documents are written, you still need to get them to your friends. How do you deal with classified **commo** between you and your co-spies? With these mad spy skills!

Document Lockdown

So, you have to bring a notebook containing the details of your newest mission to HQ for a meeting. Or maybe you're carrying your diary, or some secret letters from a friend. Whatever the case, you'd better use your binder lock for protection. Make sure you don't leave your notebook unattended. Given enough time, no lock is secure.

For Your Eyes Only

Looking for another great way to send and receive secret notes? Start a notebook of secret messages and pass it back and forth with a friend. Use your lock to keep your secrets safe and give your friend the other key.

Concealment Devices

Where else can you hide messages that you're trying to transport? Great concealment devices are often everyday objects. Take a look at the things you normally carry with you. Do any of them make a good concealment device? Is there a small space behind your MP3 player case that you could use? Fold up your secret message and tuck it inside. When you see your friend, it looks like you're showing him your MP3 player, but he's really getting your secret message.

Glove Hand-Off

No one will suspect a pair of gloves or mittens contains a secret note that you're carrying with you to "hand off" to a friend! Just stash your folded secret note inside the mitten or glove. Then place it in your pocket, or put the mitten or glove on your hand with the note stuck safely inside. When you're ready to hand it off, just lend the glove to your co-spy to try on. Then give yourself a hand for another successful pass!

Minty Pass

Fold up a small note into a tiny square and place it inside a gum wrapper or in the bottom of a tin of mints. To make the delivery, simply offer your co-spy a mint. One fresh-scented note delivered!

Game Transfer

You can use a pack of cards or a small game box to hide a secret note and pass it to a friend. Simply wedge your note between a few playing cards before putting it into the box. If anyone asks, you're not carrying top-secret info—you're just always up for a quick game!

Dead Drops

Sometimes it's not safe to hand your note to another person. The enemy could be watching and waiting to pounce. When that happens, real spies use a **dead drop**—a temporary hiding spot where spies leave information or objects for a co-spy to pick up. Dead drops are often in ordinary places that would never be suspected.

Take a glance around outside and look for some great hiding spots. Remember to make sure that you can hide an object or message there until your co-spy can pick it up. You don't want to put it anywhere *too* temporary or where it might easily be moved by someone. Check out your backyard, the park, a playground, and even outside at school. Leave no rock unturned and you'll find some excellent spots. Here are a few ideas to get you thinking.

Dead Drops Outside

⇨ **Rock Drop.** Underneath a large rock is an excellent place to hide a message for a co-spy. After choosing the rock you want to use, draw a special map with directions. Make sure your map is a good one. Include as many details as you can. If there's a water fountain or a telephone pole a few feet from the rock, draw it on the map. You want to make sure your co-spy can find the dead drop. Otherwise, you'll send your co-spy on a wild goose chase.

Flower Power. A flowerbed bursting with flowers can be a great hiding place. Just place the object between the plants on the dirt. Make sure the plants are full enough to keep it hidden!

Hosed! A coiled-up hose can be a great spot to hide a message for a dead drop. Place the note beneath the coils so it's concealed. Just make sure it's not a sprinkler day!

Trash Stash. Fold up a secret note and wedge it underneath a garbage can for a down and dirty dead drop!

Dead Drops Inside

Framed! Stash a secret document behind a picture in a frame.

Cereal Snoop. 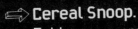 Fold up a secret note and place it in the bottom of a cereal or snack box (underneath the bag).

Sneaky Sneaker. Put something small inside a shoe or old sneaker. They'll never go digging around in there!

SPY TIP:

If you're going to use an outside dead drop, it's a good idea to put your note in a plastic baggy. That way your note will stay dry even if it stays outside for a while.

Draw the map to your dead drop using your invisible ink pens to avoid enemy interception!

Decide on a signal to let your friend know that the dead drop is ready for pickup!

Dead Drops at School

Need to dead drop a note to a friend at school? Tape a secret document to the bottom of a desk or desk drawer. Make sure your friend knows the secret signal when there's something waiting to be picked up.

Protecting the Dead Drop

Okay, so you're at school and you've hidden a secret note from one of your agents in the back of your desk. You've gotta make sure no one gets to it. What do you do? Leave it to your motion detector! Slip the juice box decoy over your alarm to transform it into an innocent-looking box of juice. Only you know what it *really* is. Next, place your little ol' juice box at the front of your desk. If a snoop decides to dig around in your desk, he'll be in for quite a shock! BEEP! BEEP! Your trusty alarm will tell him who's boss and send him running! Looks like you've caught another one!

Aldrich Ames was a **mole** who used dead drops and signals. He was a CIA officer who started spying for the Soviet Union in exchange for money. When he had new secret documents for his Soviet handlers, he would leave them at the dead drop location. Then the Soviet officers would dead drop money and instructions in return. When Ames needed to signal his Soviet handlers, he would leave a chalk mark on a mailbox.

Message Traps

If you have a sneaking suspicion that someone's been reading your secret messages, set a trap and find out for sure!

Tamper-Proof Trap

Once you seal your note, use your invisible ink pen to make diagonal marks along a fold or across the flap of the envelope. Before your friend or co-spy opens the note, she needs to check the trap by using the other end of the marker. If the lines on the note don't match up, you can bet that someone has already opened it.

Letter Lockdown

What if you get home from soccer practice and find a private letter from one of your co-spies that *wasn't* trapped? It's marked "top secret" and you know there's no better way to make curious eyes pop. Can you still check to see if anyone has opened your private mail? You betcha! Use a pair of scissors to carefully cut the envelope around the edges. Next, fill a sink with some warm water. Take the envelope and float it in the water. The envelope and flap should float apart. Let it dry (be patient—you'll have to wait a little bit for this test). Once the envelope is dry, examine the inside edges of the flap. If somebody has tampered with your mail you'll see torn fibers running along the edge.

SPY TIP:

The glue that seals envelopes is water-soluble. That means that the glue can be dissolved with water or steam, and your letter can be opened. To make your letters safer, add transparent tape to your envelope after you've sealed it. The glue on the tape won't dissolve with water!

Destroying the Evidence

What do you do with your secret notes *after* they've been read? Can you just toss them into the trash? No way! Many spies have been caught because they just crumpled up a piece of paper and chucked it into the trash. Counterspies and detectives aren't afraid of getting their hands dirty. A little garbage is well worth it if they find what they're looking for. The safest way to hide a secret message is to destroy it.

REAL SPY GADGETS

Intelligence agencies like the CIA have special machines that shred and burn their secret documents every day so there's no chance anyone will uncover their secrets.

You may think that tearing up a note into tiny pieces would do the trick—but hold on! If a counterspy is patient enough, he will piece together your secret notes. What should you do? First, tear the note into a bunch of tiny pieces. Put the pieces into different pockets and throughout the day, slowly throw them away, scattering bits of your note into different garbage cans. Now you know that no one can put your note back together, because the "puzzle pieces" aren't all in one place!

Mission
ACCOMPLISHED!

Congratulations! You've mastered the art of spy security! You know how to keep your headquarters, your stuff, and your secrets safe from prying eyes when you're at home, in school, and on the move to your next secret assignment. Those poor snoops don't stand a chance. You've even got a kit of spy gadgets to help catch anyone who dares to snoop through your stuff. You are well on your way to becoming a terrific spy!

SUZANNE FRANCIS
Writer

Suzanne writes children's books and screenplays. Her spy headquarters is in Los Angeles where she lives with her husband, Wes, and their three dogs, Belle, Lucy, and Disco.

TONY AND JONNA MENDEZ
Consultants

Tony and Jonna are retired CIA intelligence officers. They both consult for the International Spy Museum and are on its Board of Advisors. Jonna became Chief of Disguise for the CIA, and Tony once led a team to rescue six U.S. diplomats from Iran.

Glossary

Here are some spy words that you need to know:

Base of Operations – A spy's headquarters

Classified – Secret information only available to a few select people

Commo – Communication

Counterintelligence – The protection of information, people, and equipment from spies

Cover – A false identity or a fake business that spies use as a "front" to conceal their espionage

Danger Signal – A prearranged code used by a spy to alert his handlers that he has either been captured or that his cover has been blown. A danger signal can also be sent by the handler to warn a spy.

Dead Drop – A temporary hiding place used for secret exchanges between co-spies

Mole – A spy who works for one country but is secretly spying for another country

Protocol – The official method and rules agreed upon by a network of spies

Safe Site or Safe House – Temporary headquarters that a spy sets up while out of town

Spotter – A member of a counter-surveillance team who looks out for enemy surveillance

Spy Network – A group of spies who work together toward a common goal

Surveillance Detection Run or SDR – A way to find out if you're being followed

Tailing – Following somebody. If you are "tailed," *you're* being followed!

Tradecraft – The tools and tricks that spies use to collect and protect their intelligence